THE Z-D GENERATION

THE
Z-D
GENERATION

EDWARD SANDERS

STATION HILL

Copyright © 1981 by Edward Sanders. All rights reserved.

AVOID BECOMING OVERQUERULOUS!

Published by Station Hill Press, Barrytown, New York 12507. This book is issued with generous assistance from the New York State Council on the Arts and the National Endowment for the Arts, a federal agency.

Produced at Open Studio, 187 East Market Street, Rhinebeck, New York 12572. Open Studio is a non-profit design, production and training facility for writers, artists, and independent publishers, supported in part by grants from the New York State Council on the Arts and the National Endowment for the Arts, a federal agency.

ISBN 0-930794-40-0 (cloth)
ISBN 0-930794-35-4 (paper)

Manufactured in the United States of America

THE Z-D GENERATION

"This is the age of
   Investigation and every citizen must investigate"

1.   The Age of Investigation

Eleutherarchy has taken to the airwaves
since the days of Dostoevsky,
and the Freedom is there for all

Therefore, NEVER HESITATE TO OPEN
      UP A CASE FILE

      EVEN UPON THE BLOODIEST OF BEASTS
      OR PLOTS!

We will see the day of

      RELENTLESS
      PURSUIT OF DATA!

      Interrogate the Abyss!

To go after an item of time,

      (as Olson says: p. 134 of
      The Human Universe & Other Essays,

      the essence is to
      "KNOW THE NEW FACTS EARLY.")

Draw a graph or glyph
of your investigation target

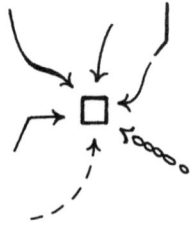

surround the glyph
with gnosis-vectors

pointing to the target

and never surrender!

Learn everything to be known
about your
data-target

then procede with Question Lists (very important
                                    to have precise,
                                      written, Q-Lists)
        toward the

                data-target

                   Δ
                   dt

Then it's robot-targeting:

if you get knocked down,
        flame-mouthed, confused by the target's
                hype or threats,

    stand up, reassemble your Q-Lists,
and proceed again toward the data-target

Holding ever in mind
The Three Adverbs

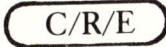

Ceaselessly/Relentlessly/Ethically.

Not that there will be no danger, though we urge the
        Three Adverbs upon you—
Just keep in mind, when targeting, say a possible
national security psychotic killer hidden in a tweed suit,

    St. Augustine's dictum,

very suitable to remember,
stress-questioning hostile data-sources:

    "The wicked persecute
    the good w/ the blindness
    of the passion that animates them,
    while the good pursue the
    wicked with a wise discretion"[1]

---

1. For more on the techniques of data-targeting, see *Investigative Poetry*, City Lights Books, 1976

The secret campaigns
of the FBI in recent
years encouraged Secret Sadism.

No more Secret Sadism!

The FBI, Military Intelligence,
The CIA, the dour minions
of National Security w/ repressionist
psyches,

must be confronted, infiltrated, exposed,
and transformed.

Art, Psychology, Openness, Love, Bravery,
and Relentlessness—

these are our tools.

Not just
Investigation,
but
Infiltration—

Demand to infiltrate the National Security grouch apparatus!

Poets, union organizers, academics, environmentalists, people of all persuasions, must demand to join, to observe, to participate in, councils of the military, councils of the police, and organizations of the right, in order to come into contact with the War Caste.

All poets and writers should
occasionally take on an investigation
that requires close scrutiny of, and contact
with, the police.

Don't be only an image in a dossier.[2]

And do not be beaten away from the barricades of investigation by fear, by shyness, by stonewall, or by the glowerings of National Security grouches.

---

2. Demand to know and to talk with the police—investigate th' investigators. Demand to know the technology, the techniques, and the personal philosophies of the secret police. Demand citizen input during working hours in the offices of the National Security Agency, say, as well as your local Sheriff's office intelligence division, not to mention the Office of Naval Intelligence, and the Pentagon's weapons research laboratories. And why should not groups of United States Citizens be drawn by lot for inspection of the nation's *most sensitive top secret* documents, plans, and proposals? And why do we not see women high in the councils of the War Caste yet? Why should not, during an interim period, a delegation from the National Organization for Women serve on the National Security Council, and have a seat on the Joint Chiefs of Staff?

2. The War Caste

I believe there grew up in this country a Warrior Caste, staffed in great part by the aging men of derring-do of War II, and now by the younger generation of Korea, Cuba, Santo Domingo, Vietnam, Chile, and Watergate—both civilians and military, mostly men, but with a few women, that is baleful and rigid, even cruel and murderous, in its rightist orthodoxy.

This generation will fade soon, and even now waxes biologically phased, leaving behind a mountain of malignant memories,
>of microfilms of malevolence,
>assassinatious gore-prints in
>wounded computers
>like a predator's paw prints
>in a snow bank.

The question is, will the men whose psyches are encased in jack boots be allowed to pass the Torch into the next millenium? Was the torch of evil, of Hitler and Mussolini, passed into the hands of American military intelligence, and into the hands of elements of the O.S.S., and thence to the hands of the CIA and the nuclear security apparatus? War trains the covert killer, and the killer of subtle mind, and sometimes one believes that because of the training in covert operations in WW II, the Cold War, Southeast Asia, South America, and so on, the War Caste will hold sway through threat of domestic murder, at least till 2000 A.D., unless this generation arises to confront and to transform.

>"But isn't everything hopeless?" you ask.
>Not at all. Nobody wants a KGB in the U.S.

> Having a country run by a
> police state is like trying
> to make a telephone call
> while wedged into a booth
> with a puking drunk.

"But, is not the poison of Hitler, Stalin, the Spartan Crypteia, the Russian Okrana, and Fascism, fully passed on to the dour minions of National Security?" you ask again.

Indeed, when one studies the secret police of Ancient Egypt, the Crypteia of Sparta (one of the worst secret polices of all time), the English police's response to the French Revolution, the Russian Okrana, the lives of poets in the Soviet Union (from Pushkin to Vosnesensky), and the illegalities of the American CIA and FBI, one begins to wonder

if a police state, as a part of the
natural human order, isn't always huddled
over the hilltop

> trying to make you believe
> it's the Dawn.

There are those who
always confuse a rigid, authoritarian state
with the
    ῥοδοδάκτυλος Ἠώς, the Rhododaktulos Eos
or rosy-fingered dawn that Homer sang about.

"We are the Dawn!
We are the Dawn!
We are the Dawn!" chant the purple-knuckled
partisans of crypto-kill,

to whom the rubicund solar blush
is the Death-ray-fingered Sun-grenade.

Many are afraid of the Secret Police:
"Oh, they'll open up a file on me! They'll
ruin me! No job, no money, no hope!"

I say, let them open up
a million files on us.

But let us open up
a million files on them too.
The technology of data-collection
is equally available
to democratic forces everywhere,
not only to the minions of pink-tracing[3],
black-listing, and robo-wash.

The hard-asses, and the
uptights, and the Ice Minds
are as interesting to
open up files on
as anybody
on the liberal left ever was.

---

3. Pink-tracing, where secret police scour your life looking for arrests in anti-war rallies, past membership in S.D.S., having taken part in student unrest, say, at 1968 Columbia, etc. In some countries, a pink-trace in your record will cost you employment, and keep you under dossier-attention, plus deny you input into national security decisions.

Plus this: inside the War Caste there are thousands
of redeemable men and women of honor striving for
perfection. There lies the only hope the world will
not be destroyed by nuclear and death-ray technology.

Open up the War Caste! Enter the War Caste!
Do not pay too much attention to the Okrana-philes,
but look for the Open Minds. Your presence will
allow them to be more assertive. Invite them
to your sing-joys! To your garden parties. Mix
your lives with theirs.

Don't be just a leaflet in a computer.

But, as to the war criminals, the assassins in tweed suits, the men
and women of the *Great Boring Burn-out Brigade* (AKA The
Association of Retired Intelligence Officers), they should be
allowed gracefully to age and to die in peace.

> Let them biologically
> phase from puissance & power,
> but as they fade,
> demand their secrets,
> seize their secrets, rip open their
>   filing cabinets!
> wade into their computers
> and view every stream!

There will even be measures of placid amusement for you, en-
countering on occasion the sort of retired soft-face

      robots with exalted security clearance
      who'll soft-rivet you w/ their
      best National Security
      glass-eyed stare,
      & tell you

William Colby is probably
a Russian mole. You laugh! But,

      in a way many of them
      in the War Caste
      were Russian moles:

      loving the up-tight Russian mode
      of repression, aping the KGB,
      loving the thrill of control and
      surveillance.

      Such are not of the ballot box
      or of the town meeting.

3. The Phenomenon of the Right Wing Nut

Many of the
National Security grouches,
the flame-mouths of secrecy,
the racists in high places,
the men and women of crypto-kill
and their dull, unimaginative, paper-pushing
slaves

    are
    subsumed beneath
    the banners of the

Right Wing Nut.

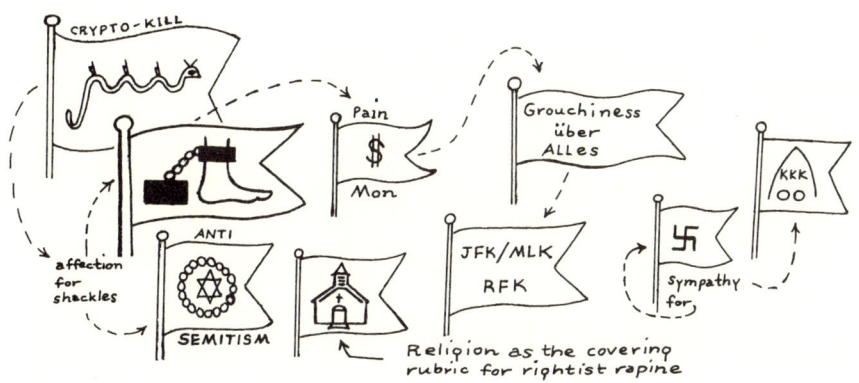

The Right Wing Nut in its heart of hearts wearies of the concept
        of voting, and longs for a rigid boss with
        powers of Total Spank

The Right Wing Nut itself is rigid, like a bazooka shell striking a tank's side, never giving up, piercing, ripping 24 hours a day, as eager to harm & to loot in the dawn as it is in the dusk.

The Right Wing Nut never knows itself wrong. Wrong is the Other. Wrong is something in the Other. Wrong never confuses it, for Wrong is a weaker mammal w/ a bullet in it.

The Right Wing Nut will slime its way into the confidence of police and intelligence, ever seeking access to, and input to, police information systems and attitudes, offering its services as crazed informants or provocateurs.

The Right Wing Nut is a voyeur of violent gossip and bad news. The r.w.n. grovels in dossiers of dirt. It loves without reason the "slimy universe of pain."

The Right Wing Nut thirsts to kill, to fire a gun, to urge others to kill, and to steal money from the oppressed while in the act of injuring the oppressed. The r.w.n. wants ironically to oppose and to propose street-gore, but more than anything to hear news about it.

The Right Wing Nut while haunted w/ an irrational hatred of blacks & minorities, yet has an awe of the prowess of the oppressed, and confuses its own hatred and rage with an imagined rage and vengeance from its victims.

The Right Wing Nut cools his fantasies on Sunday mornings in
church. Church is the calm-down ointment of
the r.w.n. Thus calmed, the right wing nut
will look into the eyes of another r.w.n., &
will know of one thing to do at once:
"Acquire Pain-Mon!" That is, the money of
rent-gouging, of migrant workers junk-food
company stores, of mafia heroin protected by
government intelligence, of war profiteering,
of gun sales to muggers, of leg-breaking to
collect debts, of bribery for quick bucks, of
hurting those whom you rip off. Selling fake
cancer drugs to the dying is the triumph of
the right wing concept of "pain-mon."

    Open up a file
    on your favorite right wing nut
    today!

      & go one-on-one
      with him or her
      in the Abyss.

    And may the drool
    dry forever on
    the lips of
    every right wing nut.

4. The Data-Midden Problem

"But, Sanders, isn't it soooo boring!?" you cry.
"All this, uh, *Data*, inelegantly arrayed in article upon article, and book after book!

And, aren't these right wing nuts you moan about ever so sleazily sleep-producing?"

Indeed, I feel sometimes
'whelmed w/ fascicles of gnarl-data!

Help! Help! Glub! Glub!
Glub-glub'd in the' Data-Midden!

as in:

> Tom Hayden's
> central FBI file
> is 250,000 pages long—
>
> Reading, say 500 pages a day, it's
> 500 days
> to read through it!
>
> But, if you make abundant
> notes as you read,
> you're down maybe
> to 250 per day:
>
> $2^5/_7$ years to read!
>
> **Help!**

Yet, what a lure is the secret workings of the U.S. gov't!

"The more people who get at the inner workings
of the system, the more information will leak, and
this will encourage countermeasures and litigation,"

> wrote Joseph Meyer, an official of
> the National Security Agency, in an
> article advocating the use of a computerized transponder system to track
> the whereabouts of arrestees, parolees,
> and multiple offenders.

Heh, heh, heh! Get at the inner workings!
> Ah, how we writhe in mirth & joy
> to get at the secret workings!

Heh, heh, heh!

And, as to the problem of the Data-Midden & Boredom,
Elutherarchy must use all the tools of art
to present its case.

> Full-color Flow Charts — the Art of the Elegant
> Footnote — 3-D Data-Grid Hologram J'Accuses —
> Investigative Poetry — A Total Pickle Fork for
> every Kernel of Discovery —

the molding of the
Carlylian "dryasdust" [4]

into items
of beauty.

Another name for the Diogenes Liberation Squadron
of Strolling Troubabdors and Muckrakers is

The **Z-D** *Generation.*

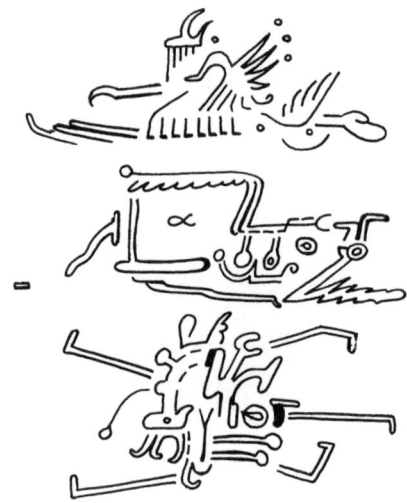

---

4. Carlylian Dryasdust. Referring to the "dryasdust" historical data-heaps through which Thomas Carlyle had to plow in order to write such books as *The Life & Letters of Oliver Cromwell,* or *Frederick the Great;* with Prussian Dryasdusts proving ever as odious to work through as Puritan Dryasdusts.

5. A New Generation

We propose the creation of

> The Z-D Generation.

Z-D! Z-D! Z-D!

ZOLA-DIDEROTS!

Émile Zola, Denis Diderot
both concerned

with the PRECISE, IMMEDIATE
application of *DATA*
of *Historical Reality,* of *Encyclopedic Wisdom*

in its own time
AS IT HAPPENS,

in correcting
the drift of a particular civilization.

10,000 Z-D's will save America!

The Zola-Diderot Generation
will fashion
a complex

of J'Accuses and Encyclopedic Paradigms
which overcome
the taunts & onslaughts
of the War Caste.

The Z-D's march
beneath the banner of the *Harsh Sophoclean Light*

The Z-D's march
beneath the banner of *Exposure of the War Caste*

The Z-D's march
beneath the banner of *Civilian Control*

The Z-D's march
beneath the banner of *Personal Freedom*

The Z-D's march
beneath the banner of *Economic Justice*

Some specific areas for the Z-D's would be

1. crack the JFK/MLK/RFK cases
2. fashion
the *Encyclopedia of 20th Century War Criminals*
3. Municipal Power, Low Cost Housing, Food Co-ops, the crushing of the rip-off will of the phone company, universal health care, the end to nukes, the triumph of Solar Power, and penny-a-page photocopying for all!

Another Z-D project
would be a thirty-volume *Encyclopedia of 20th Century American War Criminals* (to include evil scientists, robo-washers, intelligence agency assassins, war profiteers, and techno-fascists), which, if properly researched & published, and given relentless distribution and media exposure, could have a profound effect on the course of the civilization.

A measure of the potential strength of the Z-D Generation lies in the lives of Emile Zola and Denis Diderot:

> Denis Diderot
> 1713-1784
>
> The Triumph of Relentlessness
> in matters of *Keeping Issues Alive*

Born 10/5-1713
educated by Jesuits, then risked
paternal pissoff by

> "vagabond life of a
> booksellers hack in Paris"

rather than law or medicine.

Like Coleridge, Diderot attracted a circle
of admirers as prodigious talker and daring thinker.

As of $,
he worked as translator, then wrote book
of short stories, eros, Bijoux indiscrets
                    (1748)

Next wrote/published Lettre sur les aveugles
                    (1749)

a philosophical examination of rationality
for which he was
stomped into the slams
for three months

When he was released
Diderot began his giant
Encyclopaedia
       of current world ideas and data.

In 1750 an elaborate prospectus
announced the project

but, because of the enormous furor the *Encyclopaedia*
created, it wasn't until 1772 when
subscribers received final volumes

       (22 years!)

"These twenty years
were to Diderot years not
merely of incessant drudgery,
but of harassing persecution,
of sufferings from the cabals of
enemies, and of injury from the
desertion of friends."

       (from 11th Ed. Encyclopedia
       Britannica, also quotes to follow)

Spirit of free inquiry, of tolerance,
of free speculation, of democracy

       permeated Diderot's Encyclopaedia,

offending rightist death-breaths and the
Ecclesiastical Party.

After the 7th Volume was published, in 1759
the Encyclopaedia was formally suppressed.

However, the gov't became distracted
as gov't's always tend to become,
& the project was able to be continued.

"The work went on,
but with its difficulties
increased by the necessity
of being clandestine....

For seven years he labored
like a slave at the oar..."

Colleagues deserted him.
Diderot himself researched and wrote
several hundred articles for it —

wore out his eyesight
correcting proofs —

"He was incessantly
harassed all the
time by alarms of a

descent from the police."

But Diderot prevailed, conquered the death-breaths,
      through

(C/R/E)

though he was scorned by academia —
In his old age, in order to raise dower
for his daughter, had to sell his
library

(bought by Catherine the Great)

Such is the sort of life
which could afflict who truly seek to
create the *Encyclopedia of Twentieth Century War Criminals.*

Émile Zola!
1840-1902

—a best-selling novelist, at the peak of his career,
 shifts course w/ Relentless Investigation
 of the corrupt French Military.

It was as if Hemingway had stayed alive to
tackle the JFK case on every level.

      In 1894
a spy — cleaning woman,
her job was to pick up the contents
of German military attaché's waste paper basket
for the French; she found piece of paper

in handwriting of someone offering secrets
to Germans

      The French military counterintelligence felt
the handwriting was similar to an officer
      named Alfred Dreyfus; then

      anti-Semitism took over. Military forged and
lied and cheated to frame Dreyfus, even after
they learned the real identify of the traitor,
      a man named Esterhazy.

      In Dreyfus' first trial the
military produced a "secret dossier" #

so secret indeed it could not be
shown to either Dreyfus or to his
attorney

\# Was it like the secret dossier given the judge by the gov't in the Karen Silkwood civil suit?

The dossier was a cheating forgery
made by an officer in counter-intelligence,

as ugly a forgery as later
E. Howard Hunt's
fake diplomatic cables
trying to link JFK
to the killing of Diem.

Zola learned of the scam, and
He and others mounted a public campaign to free
Dreyfus, who had been sent to Devil's Island.

He worked relentlessly: blizzards of words, articles,
                            meetings, plans

The government still scammed and lied and hyped and covered
up—it was as scurrilous as the
    cover-up of the 1960's assassinations.

Zola challenged the military with his famous

                "J'Accuse"
          printed on 1/13/'98
              in L'Aurore

The military, raging faces jutting above mufti,
brought him into court—

>   And the anti-Semitic gunge
>   arose in the streets, inflamed
>   by right wing nut newspapers.

At his trial: he went to lunch under a police escort

> "Down with Zola! Down with the Jews!"
>   the anti-Semite bully-pus chanted
>   outside the courthouse.

After a court day, Zola was not allowed to return home
            directly, but went first to a friend's home,
staying for an hour or so, until those shrieking with
            hate had dispersed from in front of his house.

>   Zola lost case on first round; sentenced to year in
>   jail, and a fine, the maximum sentence;
>   which was reversed on a technicality.

At second trial, the anti-Semites still waited for him
in the streets. His motions had to be unprepared, and
nonrepeating, like someone trying to avoid a mafia hit.

He had a gun-carrying bodyguard.

Near the end of the 2nd trial, in 1898, Zola went into
exile to England for a year—

>   Dreyfus was not finally cleared until 4
>   years after Zola's death in 1902.

Robot-targeting—never give up—eat at
the barricades with an ant's tooth saw,
if that's all you have, but

never stop!

In a data-retentive era, a computer image
of the hand of Lady Macbeth is forever retained.

What remains for someone truly compiling the
*Encyclopedia of 20th Century American War Criminals,
Evil Scientists, Robo-Washers, Intelligence Agency
Assassins, War Profiteers, and Techno-Fascists,*

may well be grim. The howling anti-Semitic mobs
awaiting Zola at court is an example for anyone aptly
presenting the slide show of Bitter Revelation
                                      on the War Caste.

Zola's bodyguard had to carry a pistol

    Keep the issues alive!

The Dreyfus case lasted from 1895 till 1906. 11 years!

    Keep the issues alive!

The data-retentive era will protect us

    Keep the issues alive!

The Z-D Generation will be founded on three
living principles wrought from the lives
of Zola and Diderot:

   1. to measure
              garbage-grids,
                rails, sneers, put-downs,
    & obloquy as nothing

   2. to refuse the proffer'd hemlock
                with a
            laugh of Ha Ha Hee [5]

   3. to worship the Motto, borrowed
           from Zola,
      & transformed for our time:

> **Nulla dies
> sine linea**
>
> et
>
> Investigatione

Go on, drink the "urn of bitter prophecy," Z-D's!
And, seeing the possible future,
race into it as if you were Botticelli.

---

5. See William Blake's *Laughing Song*, from Songs of Innocence.

DESIGNED BY THE AUTHOR
IN COLLABORATION WITH SUSAN QUASHA
& THE OPEN STUDIO STAFF
THE TEXT WAS SET IN
JANSON, CLOISTER, CLOISTER OPEN FACE,
FOLKWANG, & PALATINO SEMIBOLD
WITH DRAWINGS BY THE AUTHOR
CREATED FOR THIS EDITION
PRINTED & BOUND AT OPEN STUDIO
INCLUDING FIFTY COPIES NUMBERED, SIGNED
& SPECIALLY BOUND